WOMEN'S BIBLE STUDIES

by Ruth Spradley

STANDARD PUBLISHING
Cincinnati, Ohio   39931

Library of Congress Cataloging-in-Publication Data

Spradley, Ruth.
  Women's Bible studies, Philippians.

  1. Bible. N.T. Philippians – Text-books. I. Title.
BS2705.5.S67 1987   227'.6'0076   86-23003
ISBN 0-87403-231-8

To Janet Joy Hawblitzel,
My friend, "sister" and kindred heart—
Truly "God's gracious gift" of joy to my life.
—Proverbs 27:17

PREFACE

Purpose and Use of This Study

When we want to know a person better, we have to spend time with her. We have to listen to her words and heart, asking questions to clarify things we don't understand. To the extent we listen, interact and spend time with someone, to that extent we come to know the person. The same is true in our relationship with God. We must listen to Him, interact with Him, spend time with Him. But with God we must go one step further. We must also obey Him if we are to know Him and have a growing relationship with Him (John 14:21).

Purpose

This study has been written to assist you in coming to know God better and to help you in your relationship with Him. The beautiful result in your life from such knowing and growing will be transformation into His image (2 Corinthians 3:18).

Basic Format

Each lesson has been divided into five studies (like five "devotionals") to encourage you to spend time daily with God in His Word. Each section follows a basic format to help you listen to what God says in His Word and to interact with Him and to respond to Him.

First, each study begins with a general reading of the whole passage being studied (approximately 10-12 verses). This helps you to remember the entire context before zeroing in on the verses.

The questions that follow usually proceed in a simple progression. They are designed to answer the following basic questions:

1. What are the basic facts or statements of the verse or verses? What does this verse say? (Observation.)

2. What do these facts mean? (Interpretation.) This may include definitions, thoughts from other Scriptures, comparisons with other passages, illustrations from the Old Testament, etc.

3. What do these truths mean to me? (Personalization.) These are the times to stop and meditate on the truths learned. Chew on them a little, talk with God about them, seeking His wisdom and insight.

4. What is my response to these truths, to God? (Application.) This can take a variety of forms.

    a. Praise and thanks to God for who He is and what He's done based on the truths learned.

    b. Confession of sin when you have not lived in light of the truths of Scripture (1 John 1:9). This is an important time. Often when we see our failure in light of God's truth, we respond in one of two ways:

> (1) We pass it off as impossible to achieve, so therefore we don't have to take it seriously, or
>
> (2) We get down on ourselves for our failure and walk around depressed under a load of guilt.

But God's way is neither of these. He desires a humble heart willing to confess sins and to accept His forgiveness, a heart that can experience His power as we step-by-step learn obedience to Him. (Though it may seem like we take "three steps forward and two steps back.") Remember, God knows your weaknesses, and He is merciful to you. He is also committed to working His truth into your experience (Psalm 103:10-14; Romans 8:29; Philippians 2:13).

    c. Practical steps you can take to be obedient to God's Word.

Practical Consideration

1. The questions in this study are based on the New American Standard Version.
2. When verses are listed vertically, an answer is to be found in each passage.
3. When Scriptures are listed horizontally, the truths from the passages are to be taken as a whole. A summary answer is desired.
4. Cross-references (cf.) are in parentheses and are optional. They either add further insight, or they are a repetition of the same truth in other verses.
5. The questions with an * are optional. Sometimes they are more difficult. They are added for the person who desires a more extensive study.

CONTENTS

6 And they passed through the Phrygian and Galatian region, having been forbidden by the Holy Spirit to speak the word in Asia;

7 and when they had come to Mysia, they were trying to go into Bithynia, and the Spirit of Jesus did not permit them;

8 and passing by Mysia, they came down to Troas.

9 And a vision appeared to Paul in the night: a certain man of Macedonia was standing and appealing to him, and saying, "Come over to Macedonia and help us."

10 And when he had seen the vision, immediately we sought to go into Macedonia, concluding that God had called us to preach the gospel to them.

11 Therefore putting out to sea from Troas, we ran a straight course to Samothrace, and on the day following to Neapolis;

12 and from there to Philippi, which is a leading city of the district of Macedonia, a Roman colony; and we were staying in this city for some days.

13 And on the Sabbath day we went outside the gate to a riverside, where we were supposing that there would be a place of prayer; and we sat down and began speaking to the women who had assembled.

14 and a certain woman named Lydia, from the city of Thyatira, a seller of purple fabrics, a worshiper of God, was listening; and the Lord opened her heart to respond to the things spoken by Paul.

15 And when she and her household had been baptized, she urged us, saying, "If you have judged me to be faithful to the Lord, come into my house and stay." And she prevailed upon us.

INTRODUCTION

Writing letters for most of us is a task we more often do in our heads than on paper. We desire to stay in contact with long distance loved ones, for they are dear to our hearts, but the hectic pace of life too often gets in the way. The urgent need of the moment tends to keep us from correspondence.

Paul is a wonderful example to us in this area. Though his life was completely full, he kept up close correspondence with his brothers and sisters in Christ whom he'd met on his missionary journeys. He didn't allow urgent needs to keep him from this important task. Some of his letters have been preserved for us in the New Testament, including Philippians.

Paul's letter to the Philippians is one of the warmest of his epistles. It oozes with the affection that bound Paul and the Philippian Christians together. From their first days of fellowship along the banks of the Gangites River, when Paul initially proclaimed Christ to them (Acts 16), until the last days of his Roman imprisonment, the

Spirit of God firmly knit their hearts together in love. Persecution had permitted Paul only a short stay with his new converts, but their love and commitment went deep and lasted his entire lifetime. The correspondence between them that has been left to us in the book of Philippians expresses the reality of that relationship.

Their love relationship began on Paul's second missionary journey. He desired to minister in Asia Minor, but God directed him to the European province of Macedonia. Paul followed his usual plan of evangelism in a new territory. He went to the leading city of the district, which in Macedonia was Philippi.

Philippi had the honor of being a Roman "colony." It was like having a "little Rome" on foreign soil. Politically it was organized like Rome, and its citizens enjoyed all the privileges of Roman citizenship—freedom from scourging, the right to appeal to Caesar, exemption from tribute, and the right of self-government to name a few. Most of its citizens were of Roman decent, since many of Caesar's veterans had retired in Philippi, and there had been much intermarriage with the native peoples.

In addition to its status as a colony, Philippi had great geographical significance. Located on the Egnation Way, the highway which tied the Roman Empire together, all peoples and goods going east and west always passed through Philippi. Paul was no exception. It was along this highway that he, Luke, Silas, and Timothy first entered the city.

In a new city, it was Paul's custom to first preach in a Jewish synagogue. Apparently in Philippi he found none. Instead, he discovered a group of

God-fearing women meeting for prayer on the riverbank outside of town. This was a unique experience for Paul. The first century was not a time of "women's rights." They were kept very much in the background. But Macedonia was an exception. There women enjoyed more freedom and prominence than anywhere else in the empire. Paul had the new experience of joining a women's prayer meeting.

Because of fierce persecution, Paul was able to stay with the Philippian believers only a short time before he moved on to Thessalonica. Luke was left behind to ground them in the truth. But the knot had been tied; their hearts were bound together with their beloved apostle. Through the months and years, they were fellow laborers with Paul in prayer and financial assistance. Paul on his part tried to stop and see them when he could (Acts 19:21; 20:1-6).

Philippians is a "thank-you" letter from Paul to his dear friends for one of their many gifts to him.

Besides saying a deep felt "thank you" to his friends for their generosity, Paul also shared other matters on his heart. With the verdict of his case at hand and his life hanging in the balance, he proclaimed to the Philippians, and to us as well, the joy we have in Christ, the unity we have as believers, the beauty of our Savior, and the wonderful future awaiting us with Him. These truths ring out from the depths of his soul, and they reach down deep into ours, just like they did to the Philippians so many centuries ago. They are truths which are keys to a joyful Christian life. May God deeply minister them to your life as you dig into this rich letter.

Study 1 – *Background of the Philippian Church* (Acts 16)

1. Read the introduction and Acts 16.

2. (a) Where did Paul desire to preach the gospel? (Verses 6-8)

   (b) Where did God want Paul to preach? (Verses 9 and 10)

   (c) What was Paul's response? (Verses 10-12)

   *(d) Trace Paul's itinerary as related to verses 6-12 on a large Bible map of New Testament times or in the back of your Bible.

   (e) What effect did the events of Acts 16:6-12 have on the spread of Christianity in the world?

3. (a) How did the Philippian church get started? (Verses 13-15)

   (b) How did Lydia come to believe Paul's message? (Verse 14)

4. (a) What did you discover about God from the things you've learned in questions 2 and 3?

   (b) What did the new converts learn about God from the events of Acts 16:16-40?

   (c) Meditate on the truths you've learned in 4a and 4b. Praise and thank God for who He is.

   (d) How has your view of God grown from what you've learned today?

*5. (a) What principles of practical Christian living do you discover from the events of Acts 16:13-40?

   (b) Prayerfully meditate on these truths (5a). Which one(s) do you need to apply to your life? Why? How?

   (c) Which one(s) does your husband/friend/child need in their life? Pray for them in this area.

   (d) How could you begin to teach your child the principle(s) he/she needs? (Ask God to give you insight.)

Study 2 – An Overview of Philippians

1. Read the letter to the Philippians through in one sitting.

2. What stood out to you?

*3. What did you discover about Paul and the Philippians' relationship?

Study 3 – *The Writer*

1. Go back and read Philippians 1:1, 2.

2. Who wrote the letter?

3. Describe the writer.

4. (a) Look up the following verses about bond servants. Apply what you learn to being a bond servant of Christ.

    Psalm 123:2

    Malachi 1:6

    Matthew 8:9 (cf. Luke 17:7-10)

    Matthew 10:24, 25

    Luke 12:42-44 (cf. Matthew 25:14-30)

    Luke 16:13

    (b) What further insights do the following verses give you about being Christ's bond servant?

    2 Corinthians 4:5

    Galatians 1:10

    2 Timothy 2:24, 25a

(c) Prayerfully meditate on the truths you've learned.

(d) What impressed you about being a bond servant?

Why?

(e) How do these truths need to affect your life in Christ?

*5. (a) How is being a bond servant of Christ also following in His footsteps?

Isaiah 42:1; Mark 10:45; John 13:12-17; Philippians 2:5-8

(b) Praise and thank Christ for His life and His example.

Study 4 – *The Recipients* (1:1)

1. Look again at Philippians 1:1, 2.

2. (a) The Greek word for saint means "holy one." Because a believer is "in Christ," he/she is holy in Him (separated from sin).

   (b) How are Christians "saints" or "holy" in Christ Jesus?

   Romans 6:3-11

   1 Corinthians 6:19 (cf. 1 Corinthians 3:16)

   2 Corinthians 5:17, 21

   Titus 2:14

   Hebrews 9:14

   (c) Meditate on these truths. Ask God to make them real to you. Praise and thank Him for who you are in Him.

   —If you've never accepted Christ's gift of salvation, do it now (John 1:12; Romans 10:9, 10).

   (d) Which truth in 2b ministered to you most? Why?

*3. (a) Because of who you are in Christ, what is to be the result in your daily life?

Romans 6:12, 13 (cf. Romans 12:1, 2)

Galatians 2:20

Ephesians 4:20-24

1 Peter 1:15

(b) How can we live like this (3a)?

Ephesians 3:16

2 Timothy 3:14-17 (cf. John 17:17; Colossians 3:16, 17)

Hebrews 3:13

Hebrews 12:10, 11

Study 5 – *The Greeting* (1:2)

1. Again read Philippians 1:1, 2.

2. Paul begins his letter with a salutation as was customary in his day. The normal Latin greeting was "Good Health," the Greek was "Joy," and the Hebrew was "Peace." Paul gives the Christian greeting of "Grace," and he adds to it the "Peace" of his Jewish background, which had deepened in its significance in his Christian conversion. "Grace" is God's sovereign, undeserved favor, gifts, and kindnesses in Christ. "Peace" is the result of grace in the believer's life—peace with God (reconciliation) and the peace of God (experiential).

*3. (a) Who is the source of grace and peace? (Verse 2)

(b) What do you learn about the grace and peace from God *our Father* from the prodigal son's father?
Luke 15:11-32

(c) Meditate on the insights you've gained. Praise and thank God for His grace and peace. What ministered to you most from these truths?

3 I thank my God in all my remembrance of you,

4 always offering prayer with joy in my every prayer for you all,

5 in view of your participation in the gospel from the first day until now.

6 For I am confident of this very thing, that He who began a good work in you will perfect it until the day of Christ Jesus.

7 For it is only right for me to feel this way about you all, because I have you in my heart, since both in my imprisonment and in the defense and confirmation of the gospel, you all are partakers of grace with me.

8 For God is my witness, how I long for you all with the affection of Christ Jesus.

9 And this I pray, that your love may abound still more and more in real knowledge and all discernment,

10 so that you may approve the things that are excellent, in order to be sincere and blameless until the day of Christ;

11 having been filled with the fruit of righteousness which comes through Jesus Christ, to the glory and praise of God.

1 2 3 4 5 6 7 8 9 10 11 12

THANKSGIVING, CONFIDENCE, AND PRAYER

Philippians 1:3-11

It is customary in our society to send a thank-you note when we receive a gift. New brides bear the brunt of this custom. The gifts are needed and greatly appreciated, but all the "thank yous" can become quite a chore. It's a struggle also to make each one uniquely personal with appreciation.

In Paul's day they sent thank-you notes, too. But Paul wasn't a "short-and-sweet" man. He had a great capacity to share specifically how he appreciated those who shared in his life. He opened wide his heart to those he loved.

In beginning his thank-you letter to the Philippians, Paul expressed his great joy in them, his confidence in God's work in their lives, and one of his prayers for their growth.

May God make the truths of these verses real to your heart, and a reality in your life as you spend time with Him in His Word.

Study 1 – *Paul's Thanksgiving* (1:3-5)

1. Read Philippians 1:3-11 and the introduction to this study.

2. (a) What was Paul's response when he thought about the Philippians? (Verses 3 and 4)

   (b) Why did he feel this way (2a) about them? (Verse 5)

   (c) How had the Philippians "participated" in the gospel?

   Acts 16:14, 15, 31-34

   Philippians 4:14-16

   2 Corinthians 8:1-5 (cf. Romans 15:26)

3. (a) What do the following verses tell you about Paul's prayer life and ministry? Romans 1:8-10; Ephesians 1:15, 16; Colossians 1:3, 4; 1 Thessalonians 1:2, 3; 2 Timothy 1:3, 4; Philemon 4, 5

   (b) What area of ministry has God given you?

(c) Prayerfully consider what you have learned from Paul's prayer life and ministry. How can you apply it to the ministry God has given you?

*4. (a) Look at the following prayers of Paul and pray them for those to whom you minister.
Romans 10:1; 2 Corinthians 13:7, 9; Ephesians 1:15-19; 3:14-21; Philippians 1:9-11; Colossians 1:9-12; 2 Thessalonians 1:11, 12

(b) How are Paul's prayers different from your usual prayers?

Study 2 – *Paul's Confidence* (1:6)

1. Read Philippians 1:3-11 again.
2. Define confident.

3. (a) What is the "good work" Paul's talking
       about in verse 6?
       Ephesians 2:4-10

   (b) Who has begun this "good work" in the
       believer's life?
       Philippians 1:6

   (c) What is He now doing in the believer's
       life? (Verse 6)

   (d) When will the "good work" be com-
       pleted? (Verse 6)

   (e) How will it be completed?
       Romans 8:23 (cf. Philippians 3:21)

4. What is the "day of Christ Jesus"?
       1 Thessalonians 4:16, 17;
       2 Thessalonians 1:10

5. (a) How does God perfect His work of salva-
       tion in us?

       Hebrews 12:5-7, 10, 11
       James 1:2-4 (cf. Romans 5:3-5; 1 Peter
       1:6, 7)
   (b) Why does He perfect His work in us?

       Romans 8:29

Hebrews 12:6 (cf. Romans 8:37-39)
Hebrews 12:10
1 Peter 1:7

6. (a) Meditate on the truths you've discovered today.

(b) Write out 1:6, substituting your own name.

(c) Now read your personalized version aloud several times. Ask God to make the truth sink in.

(d) Praise and thank God for His commitment to you.

(e) How has your understanding and/or appreciation of God's work in you grown from today's study?

(f) If you've never accepted Christ as your Savior, why not do so today?
John 1:12; Romans 10:9, 10

*7. (a) Why is Paul so confident that the "good work" of our salvation will be completed?
John 10:28, 29
Romans 8:29, 30
Romans 8:38, 39
Romans 11:29
1 Thessalonians 5:23, 24 (cf. Psalm 138:8)
1 Peter 1:3-5

(b) Praise and thank God for these wonderful truths. How do they encourage your heart?

Study 3 – *Paul's Heart* (1:7, 8)

1. Read Philippians 1:3-11.

2. (a) What evidence(s) of God's working in the Philippians' lives had Paul experienced? (Verse 7) Also see Study 1, question 2c.

   (b) How had their lives together in Christ affected Paul's heart toward them? (Verses 7 and 8)

3. (a) What is the "affection of Christ Jesus" that Paul felt for the Philippians?

   Matthew 23:37

   John 10:11-15

   John 15:9, 17:24

   2 Corinthians 8:9

   (b) Why could Paul have Christ's affection for the Philippians?
   Galatians 2:20

   (c) What impressed you most about the affection between Christians you discovered in 3a and 3b? Why?

4. How does the relationship of Paul and the Philippians illustrate the reality of what Christ prayed for in John 17:20-23?

5. (a) Meditate on the things you've learned. Praise and thank Christ for His love and for how it binds you together with other believers.

   (b) Evaluate your relationship with your minister/church members/missionaries in light of what you've learned about Paul and the Philippians. What changes need to be made?

*6. How does Paul's expression of his heart in Philippians 1:3-8 show the reality of what he taught in Romans 12:4, 5 and 1 Corinthians 12:12-27?

Study 4 – *Paul's Prayer* (1:9)

1. Once again read Philippians 1:3-11.

2. Though the Philippians had shown Christ's love to Paul over and over, what is his prayer for them? (Verse 9)

3. Define abound.

4. (a) How important is love?
        1 Corinthians 13:1-3

    (b) Who are we to love?
         Matthew 22:37-39 (cf. John 13:34)

    (c) What is love?
         1 Corinthians 13:4-8a

    (d) Take time to let these truths sink in. What stands out to you?

5. (a) What is the "real knowledge" that is to govern our love?

        1 John 4:7-11 (cf. Ephesians 3:18, 19)

        John 14:21-23

    (b) How does one develop a discerning love?

Romans 12:2

1 Thessalonians 5:21, 22

Hebrews 5:12-14 (especially verse 14)

*(c) What relationship do you see between "real knowledge" and "all discernment"?

6. (a) Review prayerfully the truths you've studied. Praise and thank God for His love.

(b) Pray verse 9 back to God as your personal prayer for your relationship with Him and with the significant people in your life (spouse, children, friends, etc.).

(c) How do you need to apply to your life the truths you've learned today? (Ask God for wisdom.)

*7. Give a summary statement of what it means:

(a) To love God with "real knowledge" and "all discernment."

(b) To love others with "real knowledge" and "all discernment."

Study 5 – *The Purpose and Grounds of Paul's Prayer* (1:10, 11)

1. Once more read Philippians 1:3-11.

2. (a) Why did Paul want the Philippians' love to grow in knowledge and discernment? (Verse 10)

   (b) How would love with knowledge and discernment make this (a) possible? (You may want to review Study 4.)

   (c) Why is it important?
   2 Corinthians 5:10 (cf. 1 Corinthians 3:10-15)

3. Why was it possible for the Philippians to live the kind of life expressed in verses 9 and 10? (Verse 11)

4. (a) How is a Christian righteous?
   2 Corinthians 5:21; Philippians 3:9

   (b) What is the fruit of that righteousness?

   Galatians 5:22, 23

   James 3:17, 18

   Proverbs 11:30

   (c) How does the Christian experience the fruit of righteousness in his/her life?

John 15:4, 5

Psalm 1:2, 3

(d) Why is fruit important in our lives?
John 15:8

5. (a) What was the end goal of Paul's prayer?
Philippians 1:11

(b) Why is this important?
1 Corinthians 10:31

6. Stop and think on the truths you've learned. Which truth(s) stands out to you? Why?

7. Asking God for insight, how do these truths affect your life?

12 Now I want you to know, brethren, that my circumstances have turned out for the greater progress of the gospel,

13 so that my imprisonment in the the cause of Christ has become well-known throughout the whole praetorian guard and to everyone else,

14 and that most of the brethren, trusting in the Lord because of my imprisonment, have far more courage to speak the word of God without fear.

15 Some, to be sure, are preaching Christ even from envy and strife, but some also from good will;

16 the latter do it out of love, knowing that I am appointed for the defense of the gospel;

17 the former proclaim Christ out of selfish ambition, rather than from pure motives, thinking to cause me distress in my imprisonment.

18 What then? Only that in every way, whether in pretense or in truth, Christ is proclaimed; and in this I rejoice, yes, and I will rejoice.

19 For I know that this shall turn out for my deliverance through your prayers and the provision of the Spirit of Jesus Christ,

20 according to my earnest expectation and hope, that I shall not be put to shame in anything, but that with all boldness, Christ shall even now, as always, be exalted in my body, whether by life or by death.

1 2 3 4 5 6 7
8 9 10 11 12

PROCLAIMING CHRIST

Philippians 1:12-20

Witnessing is a frightening activity to many Christians. Though Christ told His disciples that they would be His witnesses in Acts 1:8 (a witness bears testimony to certain facts and his own personal experience), the thought of telling another person about Christ leaves many terrified. So we have seminars to tell us how, programs to get us started, and pamphlets to tell us what to say. Somehow though it doesn't relieve us of the panic and pressure of "having to" witness.

Paul's life was centered in proclaiming Christ. Even in prison it was his primary focus. His prime concern was Christ's exaltation in his life, for

Christ was his life. Herein lies one of the secrets of his bold witness and one can't help but talk about what one's life is focused on.

In this lesson, we'll study the circumstances, motives, and heart attitudes in witnessing that we discover in Paul. We'll see how his focus made all the difference. We'll also take a look at the basic truths that make up the "gospel" (good news about Jesus Christ) and how to share that with another.

Then in the next lesson, we'll see in more detail how Christ was the center of Paul's life—which must be true of ours as well if witnessing is going to be a delight rather than a frightening duty.

May God open your life to witnessing of Him through your study.

Study 1 – *The Circumstances* (1:12-14)

1. Read the introduction and Philippians 1:12-20.

2. What were Paul's circumstances in verses 12 and 13? (cf. Acts 28:11-31)

3. (a) What would you think of your minister's (or a missionary's) opportunities for witnessing if he were in jail?

   (b) How do you think the Philippians felt concerning Paul's ministry when they heard he was in prison?

   (c) What did Paul want the Philippians to realize about his ministry for Christ in prison? (Verses 12 and 13)

   (d) What was the result of his imprisonment in the lives of Christians in Rome? (Verse 14)

4. (a) What truths did Paul know to focus on so that he could remain effective in his ministry in trying circumstances?

   Romans 5:3-5

   Romans 8:28

   2 Corinthians 4:11, 12

   Philippians 1:20

2 Timothy 2:9

(b) How does Ephesians 6:19, 20 help you
    understand the effectiveness of Paul's
    ministry in prison?

5. Prayerfully review what you've learned today.

6. (a) What circumstances in your life seem
       like a prison (physically, family responsi-
       bilities, etc.)?

   (b) What has been your attitude toward
       them? (If there's been sin, be sure and
       confess it to God, ask His forgiveness,
       and thank Him for His forgiveness.)

   (c) How do you need to emulate Paul in fo-
       cus and ministry?

   (d) Who is praying for your Christian wit-
       ness?

7. (a) Praise and thank God for His sovereign
       control. Thank Him specifically for your
       circumstances (Ephesians 5:20). Ask
       Him to keep your focus on His glory and
       the proclaiming of His Son. Ask Him for
       a group of praying friends to support
       you.

   (b) Today ask at least one person to pray for
       you specifically this way.

Study 2 – *The Motives* (1:15-18)

1. Again read Philippians 1:12-20.

2. In verses 15 to 17, Paul tells us about two groups of people active in evangelism in Rome. One group had pure motives, the other did not. Fill in the following chart comparing these two groups.

   Group 1 (Impure)   *Group II (Pure)*
   (a) Their Motives   (a) Their Motives

   (b) The Reason   (b) The Reason

3. Review your chart. Try to picture Paul's situation and the feelings that would go with it. Describe the situation in your own words, and how it might feel for Paul.

4. (a) What was Paul's heart's desire and focus in his situation? (Verse 18)

   (b) What was his heart attitude in the midst of this rivalry? (Verse 18)

5. (a) How do you handle situations of envy and strife?

   (b) Is your focus and purpose the same as Paul's?

(c) What changes need to be made? (Ask God for insight and wisdom.)

6. Ask God to work in you the things you wrote down in 5c. Praise and thank Him for the example of godly living He gave in Paul. Thank Him that He can do the same work in you!
Ephesians 3:20

*7. From what you know of Paul and the early church, why might some first century Christians have negative attitudes towards Paul?

*8. Compare Paul's description and reaction to the people with impure motives in Philippians 1:15-18 with his description and reaction to the Judaizers in 2 Corinthians 11:1-4, 13-15 and Galatians 1:6-9. What conclusions can you draw?

Study 3 – *The Deliverance and Exaltation (1:19-20)*

1. Read Philippians 1:12-20.

2. (a) What did Paul believe was going to happen to him? (Verse 19)

   (b) How was it going to take place? (Verse 19)

   (c) What was Paul's deep desire in all of it? (Verse 20)

*3. (a) In light of what Paul says in verse 20 about life or death, how could death be as much a "deliverance" as being set free from prison? (cf. 2 Corinthians 5:1-9)

   (b) How would the Philippians' prayers and the Holy Spirit (verse 19) be needed for either possibility?

4. Why could Paul have such a strong confidence that he would not be put to shame?

   Isaiah 50:7

   Romans 9:33

   1 Peter 4:16, 19

Ephesians 6:19, 20
Colossians 4:2-4
1 John 5:14, 15

5. Meditate on what you've studied. Praise and thank God for His trustworthiness. Ask Him to give you a heart set on His glory in every situation.

6. (a) What impressed you most in your study of this section? Why?

   (b) What desires has God implanted in your heart because of your study today (or the last three days)?

Study 4 – *The Proclamation*, Part 1 (1:18)

1. Read Philippians 1:12-20.

2. What was the overriding desire of Paul's heart? (Verse 18)

3. When sharing Christ with others, there are some foundational truths which you need to know and be able to explain. Today we'll look up some of those truths. Tomorrow you'll get the opportunity to weave them together in your own presentation of the gospel.

4. What is God like?

   1 John 4:8

   Revelation 4:8 (cf. 1 John 1:5)

   Psalm 5:4, 5

5. Who is Jesus Christ?

   John 5:18 (cf. John 10:30; 14:9)

   Hebrews 2:14a, 17a

   1 Timothy 2:5

6. What is man like?

   Mark 7:20-23 (cf. Mark 10:18; Jeremiah 17:9)

Romans 3:23

7. What is the result of sin?
   Romans 6:23

8. What is the meaning of Christ's crucifixion?

   Matthew 26:28

   1 Peter 2:24 (cf. 1 Peter 3:18; Isaiah 53:5)

9. What is the meaning of Christ's resurrection?
   Luke 24:46-48

10. Why did God send Christ to die?
    John 3:16

11. How is one saved?
    John 1:12 (cf. Acts 2:38; Romans 10:9, 10; Ephesians 2:8, 9)

12. Meditate on these truths.

    Praise and thank God for himself, His Son, and His gift of salvation.

13. If you've never come to know Christ personally, don't delay. Why not today?

Study 5 – *The Proclamation*, Part 2 (1:18)

1. Once again read Philippians 1:12-20.

2. Write in your own words an explanation of the gospel that would lead another person into a personal, saving relationship with Jesus Christ. (Use the truths you learned yesterday.)

3. Ask God for an opportunity to share the gospel with some one. Ask Him to open your eyes and keep you ready to share.

21 For to me, to live is Christ, and to die is gain.

22 But If I am to live on in the flesh, this will mean fruitful labor for me; and I do not know which to choose.

23 But I am hard pressed from both directions, having the desire to depart and be with Christ, for that is very much better;

24 yet to remain on in the flesh is more necessary for your sake.

25 And convinced of this, I know that I shall remain and continue with you all for your progress and joy in the faith,

26 so that your proud confidence in me may abound in Christ Jesus through my coming to you again.

27 Only conduct yourselves in a manner worthy of the gospel of Christ; so that whether I come and see you or remain absent, I may hear of you that you are standing firm in one spirit, with one mind striving together for the faith of the gospel;

28 in no way alarmed by your opponents—which is a sign of destruction for them, but of salvation for you, and that too, from God.

29 For to you it has been granted for Christ's sake, not only to believe in Him, but also to suffer for His sake,

30 experiencing the same conflict which you saw in me, and now hear to be in me.

LIFE AND DEATH

Philippians 1:21-30

What is "real living" to you? Inheriting a million dollars and vacationing around the world the rest of your life? That perfect home you've always dreamed of? Fulfillment of your secret dreams? Time to do what you please? Or ____ ?

To Paul "real living" was Christ himself. It was Christ's life lived out within him (Galatians 2:20; Colossians 3:3, 4a). His identity, his joy, his strength, his focus was Christ. Because of this death was gain—the chance to be face to face with Him who was his life.

This kind of living may seem impossible for you, but it's not. Paul's experience of Christ in his life and as his life can be ours as well. The truths of Scripture are not for an elite few. Ephesians 3:20 tells us God can do far more for us and in us than we can ever think or ask. Why not ask Him to work in you so that you, too, might know Christ in experience as your life?

When we begin to grasp the truth of Christ as our life and experience it, then we will be bolder in our witness—not only in what we say but also in how we live. There will be power; there will be a divine dynamic in living.

May the truths you learn in these verses sink down into your soul. As you discover (or review) who you are in Christ and what you have in Him, may you realize your worth to God in your deepest being. And as a result, may you walk worthy of your standing.

Study 1 – *Paul's View of Life and Death* (1:21)

1. Read the introduction and Philippians 1:21-30.

2. (a) Why can Paul (and any believer) say that for him "to live is Christ"?

    Galatians 2:20

    Colossians 3:3, 4a (cf. Colossians 1:27b)

    (b) Stop and meditate on this truth. Though it may be familiar, ask God to make it real to your inner being.

    (c) How do you think about yourself (your self-image)?

    (d) How is what you answered in 2c different from what you learned in 2a?

    (e) Asking the Holy Spirit for insight, how do you need to begin viewing your life in light of Galatians 2:20 and Colossians 3:3, 4a? (Be specific.)

    (f) Praise and thank God for your life in Christ and for His life in you.

3. (a) How have you viewed death?

    (b) Define gain.

(c) How is death "gain" for a Christian?

2 Corinthians 5:1, 6, 8

1 Corinthians 13:12 (cf. John 17:24)

(d) Why can death be "gain" for a Christian?
Hebrews 2:14, 15

(e) Meditate on what you've learned. Though these may be "old" truths to you, ask God to make them sink down deep inside. Praise and thank God for the "gain" of death.

(f) What ministered to you most from these truths? Why?

(g) How has your view of death changed because of today's study?

*4. Write out the meaning of Philippians 1:21 in your own words.

Study 2 – *Paul's Dilemma* (1:22-26)

1. Again read Philippians 1:21-30.
2. What is the dilemma Paul feels emotionally as he awaits the verdict on his life? (Verses 22-24)

3. (a) Why does Paul conclude that his life will be spared a while longer? (Verses 24 and 25)

    (b) What would be the result of Paul's acquittal for the Philippians? (Verse 26)

4. Why would this dilemma pull at Paul so hard in each direction?

    (a) To depart
        2 Corinthians 5:2-4 (cf. Romans 8:23)
        John 14:3 (cf. John 17:24)
    (b) To stay
        Ephesians 4:11-13 (cf. Acts 20:29-31)

5. Prayerfully review your answers. How do verses 22-26 further explain what Paul says in verse 21?

6. (a) In the last two days, what have you learned from Paul's life which you would like to have in your own?

    (b) Ask God to work what you wrote down in 6a deep into your life.
        Remember Ephesians 3:20!

Study 3 – *The Philippians' Conduct*, Part 1 (1:27a)

1. Read Philippians 1:21-30.

2. The Greek word for "conduct yourselves in a manner worthy" literally means "exercise your citizenship."

3. Why did the Philippians (and us) need to conduct themselves worthy of gospel? Philippians 3:20

4. Second Peter 1:4-9 gives us an explanation of a walk worthy of the gospel, one which exercises our citizenship. Read the passage.

5. Why are the qualities listed in 2 Peter 1:4-9 important ingredients of a walk worthy of our citizenship?

   (a) Faith—Hebrews 11:1, 6 (cf. Romans 1:16, 17)

   (b) Moral excellence—1 Peter 1:14-16 (cf. 1 Thessalonians 4:3-7)

   (c) Knowledge—Jeremiah 9:24 (cf. Proverbs 1:7)

   (d) Self-control—1 Corinthians 9:24-27 (especially verse 25) (cf. Galatians 5:23)

   (e) Perseverance—James 1:3, 4 (cf. Romans 5:3, 4)

(f) Godliness—1 Timothy 4:7, 8 (cf. 6:6)

(g) Brotherly kindness—1 John 3:16-18 (cf. Hebrews 6:10)

(h) Love—Matthew 22:37-39 (cf. 1 Corinthians 13:1-8)

(i) Meditate on these truths. What stands out to you? Why?

6. What is the result in our lives when these qualities flourish?
2 Peter 1:8

7. (a) What is God's responsibility in seeing these qualities become a reality in my daily living?
Philippians 2:13

(b) What is mine?
2 Peter 1:5a (cf. Philippians 2:12)

8. (a) Prayerfully review your answers. Praise and thank God for His gift of heavenly citizenship and for His commitment to you. Ask Him for great diligence in living out your citizenship in your everyday experience.
(b) How have these truths affected your view of the Christian life?

(c) How do these truths need to affect your life?

*9. Compare what you learned today with John 15:1-8.

Study 4 – *The Philippians' Conduct, Part 2 (1:27b, 28)*

1. Read Philippians 1:21-30.

2. What does Paul want to hear about the Philippians? (Verse 27b)

3. (a) Compare Philippians 1:27b with Ephesians 4:1-3.

    (b) How does Ephesians 4:2 explain how one can carry out Paul's desire for the Philippians in Philippians 1:27b?

    (c) Meditate on these truths. Ask God for insight into how they need to affect your life.

    (d) What insight did God give you?

4. (a) In verse 28 Paul tells the Philippians that, as they stand firm in Christ without fear in the face of opposition, their confidence is a sign of their ultimate salvation and their oppressors doom. Why is this so?

    Isaiah 51:7, 8

    2 Thessalonians 1:4-8

(b) Meditate on these truths. Praise and thank God for them. What ministered to you most? Why?

(c) Spend time praying for any Christians you know who are suffering for their faith. Then pray for believers in countries where they suffer greatly for their faith.

Study 5 – *Paul and the Philippians'*
Suffering and
Conflict (1:29, 30)

1. Read Philippians 2:21-30.

2. The word for "granted" in the Greek means to show favor or kindness. It comes from the word for "grace." It is a good gift freely given.

3. (a) What had been granted to the Philippians? (Verse 29)

    (b) What insights do these verses give you into this truth (3a)?

    Matthew 5:10-12

    Acts 5:40-42

    1 Peter 4:12-14

    (c) Meditate on these truths. Ask God to renew your mind in these truths. Praise and thank God for them. What truth touched your heart? Why?

    (d) How have these truths affected your view of suffering for Christ?

*4. (a) What was the suffering and conflict the Philippians had seen in Paul's life? Acts 16:19-40

(b) What was Paul now experiencing?
    Philippians 1:13, 17 (cf. Acts 28)

(c) How do these experiences of Paul illus-
    trate what you learned in questions 2
    and 3?

1 If therefore there is any encouragement in Christ, if there is any consolation of love, if there is any fellowship of the Spirit, if any affection and compassion,

2 make my joy complete by being of the same mind, maintaining the same love, united in spirit, intent on one purpose.

3 Do nothing from selfishness or empty conceit, but with humility of mind let each of you regard one another as more important than himself;

4 do not merely look out for your own personal interests, but also for the interests of others.

5 Have this attitude in yourselves which was also in Christ Jesus,

6 who, although He existed in the form of God, did not regard equality with God a thing to be grasped,

7 but emptied Himself, taking the form of a bondservant, and being made in the likeness of men.

8 And being found in appearance as a man, He humbled Himself by becoming obedient to the point of death, even death on a cross.

9 Therefore also God highly exalted Him, and bestowed on Him the name which is above every name,

10 that at the name of Jesus every knee should bow, of those who are in heaven, and on earth, and under the earth,

11 and that every tongue should confess that Jesus Christ is Lord, to the glory of God the Father.

UNITY AND HUMILITY

Philippians 2:1-11

The great hymns of the church have stirred the souls of God's people for centuries. At times they pick up our sagging spirits. In times of worship, they seemingly can transport us into the very throne room of God. Even in Heaven we'll sing praises to our Father and Savior (Revelations 5:9-13).

In Philippians 2:6-11, we find what many Bible scholars believe was part of a first century hymn. It is a hymn celebrating the great humility, obedience, and exaltation of Christ. Paul uses it as a teaching example for his exhortation to unity and humility among the Philippians.

It is impossible to have unity without humility. In Philippians 2:1, Paul tells us the basis for our unity as Christians, and then he exhorts us to live it out (2:2). It can only be lived out if each one of us is walking humbly with our brothers and sisters in Christ. Paul explains how we can do this in verses 3 and 4.

But explanations and exhortations are not enough. We need to see it in flesh and blood. So Paul shares with us the supreme example of humility—Jesus Christ. When we clearly see Him, there's no room for any of us to resist the exhortations of verses 1-4.

May your appreciation, worship, and adoration of Christ grow through your study of these verses. And as a result of "seeing" Him, may you be encouraged in your walk of humility and unity.

Study 1 – *Unity: Its Foundation and Practice (2:1, 2)*

1. Read the introduction and Philippians 2:1-11.

2. The "if" clauses in the first verse actually have the force of "since" in the Greek. There is certainty of these things, not doubt. Take a look at these "love gifts" of God to His children. Meditate on the truths as you go and ask Him for insight and appreciation.

3. What is the "encouragement in Christ" (verse 1) that we have?

   John 14:27

   John 16:24

   2 Corinthians 2:14

   1 Peter 1:4, 5

4. What is the "consolation of love" (verse 1) we experience?

   John 15:9, 10 (cf. Romans 5:5)

   John 15:12, 13

5. What is the "fellowship of the Spirit" (verse 1) we enjoy?

Romans 8:14-16

Romans 8:26, 27

1 Corinthians 12:13

6. What is the "affection and compassion" (verse 1) we experience and express? 1 John 3:16

7. (a) Meditate on the truths you've learned. Praise and thank God for His *great* gifts to you. Praise Him for His love.

   (b) Which truth ministered to you most? Why?

8. Because of what God's given us, how are we to live together as Christians or believers? (Verse 2)

*9. How do the truths you've learned in verse 1 (questions 3-6) make possible the life requested in verse 2?

Study 2 – *Humility in Action* (2:3, 4)

1. Again read Philippians 2:1-11.

2. In verses 3 and 4, Paul gives instruction as to specific things we are to do and not do if we are to walk in unity and humility. Fill in the following chart from verses 3 and 4. Give illustrations from your own life (positive and/or negative) where you can of these truths.

Things to do   *Things not to do*

3. (a) Prayerfully review these exhortations, asking God to convict you where needed. If He convicts you of sin (failure, disobedience), confess it to Him, ask His forgiveness, and thank Him for His forgiveness.
    (b) Ask God to work in your areas of weakness.
    (c) Is there any brother or sister in Christ or a non-Christian (spouse, child, friend, fellow worker) who has been affected by your sin (3a)? If so, be sure and confess your sin to them and ask their forgiveness also.

*4. How would living in obedience to these exhortations result in fulfilling Paul's desire in verse 2?

*5. What connection do you see between unity and humility?

Study 3 – *The Supreme Example* (2:5-7)

1. Once more read Philippians 2:1-11.

2. Who is the supreme example of the attitudes and actions expressed in verses 3 and 4? (Verse 5)

3. (a) What does it mean that Jesus existed in the form of God? (Verse 6)
     John 1:1 (cf. Colossians 1:16, 17)

   (b) How is Jesus equal with God?

     John 5:18

     John 10:30 (cf. John 14:9)

   (c) Meditate on these truths. Ask God to make real to you who Christ is and has been for all eternity.

4. (a) What things/rights/perogatives as God did Christ let go of when He came to earth?

     John 5:30 (cf. John 5:19)

     John 17:5, 24 (cf. Isaiah 6:1-3)

     2 Corinthians 8:9 (cf. 2 Corinthians 5:21)

(b) In what way did Christ empty himself?
    (Verse 7)

5. (a) Define bond servant.

   (b) How do these verses show Jesus as a
       bond servant?
       Isaiah 50:4-7 (cf. Hebrews 5:8)

   (c) How do these verses show Jesus' humil-
       ity?

       John 1:14 (cf. Isaiah 7:14; Hebrews 2:14)

6. Meditate on these truths. Ask God to make
   real to your heart Jesus' attitude in coming
   to earth for you. Praise Him and thank Him.
   How has your understanding and/or appreciation of Jesus Christ grown from your
   study?

Study 4 – *The Supreme Example*, Part 1 (2:8)

1. Read Philippians 2:1-11.

2. (a) What was Christ's ultimate expression of Philippians 2:3, 4? (Verse 8)

   (b) What do you learn about this (2a) from Isaiah 52:14 and Isaiah 53:2-8?

3. Meditate on these truths. Praise and thank Christ for His obedience unto death for you. Which truth(s) particularly touched your heart? Why?

4. (a) Reflect on the truths you've learned the last two days in light of Philippians 2:3, 4.

   (b) How has your understanding of Paul's exhortation in Philippians 2:3, 4 increased because of studying Christ's example?

   (c) Asking God for insight, how do these truths need to affect your life?

Study 5 – *The Supreme Example*, Part 2 (2:9-11)

1. Read Philippians 2:1-11.

2. In one word, what was the result of Christ's humbling himself to the point of death? (Verses 9-11)

3. What is the name above *all* names which Jesus received?

    Revelation 19:12 (cf. Revelation 3:12)
    Revelation 19:16

4. Why will every tongue confess and every knee bow to the lordship of Christ?

    Psalm 45:6, 7 (cf. Daniel 7:14; Isaiah 9:7; 1 Corinthians 15:24-27a; Revelation 11:15)
    Matthew 28:18
    Acts 5:31
    Hebrews 10:12, 13 (cf. Revelation 3:21)

5. Meditate on these truths. Worship Christ with praise and adoration. Which truth stood out to you? Why?

*6. (a) How does what you've learned of Christ in Philippians 2:5-11 exemplify what He taught in Matthew 23:12 (cf. Luke 14:11; 18:14)?

     (b) How can this (6a) be an encouragement to you in obeying Philippians 2:3, 4?

12 So then, my beloved, just as you have always obeyed, not as in my presence only, but now much more in my absence, work out your salvation with fear and trembling;

13 for it is God who is at work in you, both to will and to work for His good pleasure.

14 Do all things without grumbling or disputing;

15 that you may prove yourselves to be blameless and innocent, children of God above reproach in the midst of a crooked and perverse generation, among whom you appear as lights in the world,

16 holding fast the word of life, so that in the day of Christ I may have cause to glory because I did not run in vain nor toil in vain.

17 But even if I am being poured out as a drink offering upon the sacrifice and service of your faith, I rejoice and share my joy with you all.

18 And you too, I urge you, rejoice in the same way and share your joy with me.

1 2 3 4 5 **6** 7 8 9 10 11 12

WORKING OUT OUR SALVATION

Philippians 2:12-18

Though our salvation is totally a gift of God's grace, we are to be obedient to God's Word and alert to the Spirit's prompting. But, as a car cannot run unless it has fuel, so a Christian cannot live except by the power of God. He is the fuel for our living (Philippians 2:13).

Many Christians feel they have to work out their salvation without realizing the power source within them. Subsequently, they fail to draw on that power. Too often we're like children playing at driving parked cars. We need to realize we're licensed drivers who can push down the gas pedal and get out into traffic.

In Philippians 2:12-18, Paul reminds us of our responsibility to "get out on the road," but he also lets us know we have a *full* fuel tank for the journey. In addition, he gives us some practical pointers on how to be "good drivers."

Study 1 – *The Heart Attitude* (2:12)

1. Read the introduction and Philippians 2:12-18.

2. (a) What had been the Philippians record of obedience? (Verse 12a)

   (b) Who had helped to inspire their obedience when he was with them? (Verse 12a)

   (c) What is his concern for their obedience in his absence? (Verse 12a)

   (d) How are they to be obedient? (Verse 12b)

3. (a) How is one saved?
   Ephesians 2:8, 9

   (b) How does one work out this gift of salvation in practical, everyday living?

   John 15:4, 5

   Romans 13:11-14 (cf.1 Corinthians 9:24-27; 1 Timothy 4:7-10)

   Hebrews 12:1, 2 (cf. Matthew 11:29; 2 Peter 3:18)

   (c) Meditate on these truths. Ask God to open your eyes to how these truths have been a part of your life and how they need to be even more experienced in your life.

(d) How have you experienced these truths already?

(Praise and thank God for what He's done in you.)

(e) Which truth(s) did God impress upon your heart as one you need to begin (or grow in) practicing? How? Why?

(f) If you've never accepted God's gift of salvation, do so today (Acts 2:38; Romans 10:9, 10).

4. (a) What is to be the Christian's attitude in working out his salvation? (Verse 12b)

(b) What does this (4a) mean?
Psalm 2:11 (cf. Isaiah 66:2); Romans 8:15; Hebrews 12:28, 29

(c) Prayerfully meditate on this truth. Has this characterized your attitude in your Christian life? If not, confess it as sin to God, ask His forgiveness, and thank Him for forgiveness. Ask God for a heart of deep reverence for Him.

Study 2 – *The Power* (2:13)

1. Again read Philippians 2:12-18.

2. Why can you work out your salvation in your practical living? (Verse 13)

3. (a) Who is this God who works in you as a Christian?

    1 Chronicles 29:11, 12

    Jeremiah 32:17

    (b) Stop and meditate on who your God is. Let it really sink in. What stands out to you? Why?

    (c) In what area of your Christian life does it seem impossible for you to experience victory (walk consistently in obedience)?

    (d) How have you felt about your failure (disobedience) in this area?

    (e) What do Jeremiah 32:17 and Philippians 2:13 tell you about this area of your life?

    (f) Thank God for this truth in relation to your specific area of weakness. Thank Him for what He is doing and is going to do. How has your heart been encouraged?

(g) Whenever you fail in this area, be sure to confess it as sin to God. Ask His forgiveness and thank Him for it. Thank Him for the process of conforming you to the image of Christ. Thank Him for His commitment to you.

4. (a) Why does God work in us? (Verse 13)

(b) Praise and thank God for His love toward you.

*5. Explain the Christian life from what you've learned in Philippians 2:12 and 13.

Study 3 – *The Practice and Proof of Our Salvation (2:14, 15)*

1. Read Philippians 2:12-18.

*2. (a) What command do you discover in Philippians 2:14?

   (b) Why are we to be obedient in this (2a) way? (Verse 15)

3. The Jews who left Egypt with Moses are a negative example of Paul's exhortation in Philippians 2:14, 15. They were to be God's light to the world. Let's take a look and see what we can learn from them (1 Corinthians 10:6-12).

   (a) What had been God's promise to the Jews?
   (Exodus 6:6-8)

   (b) What were their attitudes and actions as they journeyed to the promised land?

   Exodus 14:10-12

   Numbers 11:1 (cf. Numbers 14:1-4; Numbers 20:2-5; Numbers 21:4, 5)

   (c) How did Moses characterize them?
   Deuteronomy 31:27

4. (a) What are God's promises to you? (You may want to add others.)

Romans 8:28-30

Romans 8:38, 39

Philippians 1:6

Philippians 4:19 (cf. Matthew 6:25-32)

(b) What are the things you complain about or dispute over?

5. Review all you've learned today.

(a) How are you like the Jews under Moses?

(b) How might God characterize you?

(c) Confess to God as sin any grumbling, disputing, or rebellion. Ask His forgiveness and thank Him for it.

(d) Thank God for His promises. Which one do you need to memorize and think on daily to combat your area(s) of complaining?

*6. How does grumbling and disputing keep you from being a light to your world?

Study 4 – *The Place of the Word* (2:16)

1. Once more read Philippians 2:12-18.

2. One of the ways we shine as lights in this world (2:15) is by centering on God's Word. In verse 16 we are seen as "holding fast" or "holding forth" the Word of Life. The Greek word can be translated either way.

3. What is the "Word of Life?"
    John 6:68 (cf. John 1:4); Hebrews 4:12

4. (a) How do we "hold fast" the Word?

    Psalm 119:11

    Colossians 3:16

    2 Timothy 2:15

    1 Peter 2:2

    (b) Review your answers prayerfully. Which truth(s) stand out to you? Why?

    (c) Asking God for insight, which truth in 4a do you need in your life to hold fast the Word? Why? How?

    (d) Ask God to put this deep into your heart and life. Praise and thank Him for what He's going to do (Ephesians 3:20).

5. (a) How are we to "hold forth" the Word of
       Life?

       Matthew 5:16

       Matthew 28:19, 20 (cf. 2 Corinthians
       5:18-20)

       1 Peter 3:15

   (b) Prayerfully think on these things. What
       stands out to you? Why?

   (c) Asking God for insight, how do these
       truths need to affect your life?

   (d) Ask God to put these things deep into
       your living pattern. Praise and thank
       Him for what He's going to do.
       (Ephesians 3:20).

6. How would the Philippians obedience to
   Philippians 2:14-16a affect Paul's life?
   (Verse 16b)

7. Praise and thank God for the Word of Life.
   Thank Him for the privilege of holding it
   "fast" and "forth." Remember Philippians
   2:13.

Study 5 – *The Offering of Our Lives* (2:17, 18)

1. Read Philippians 2:12-18.

2. In verse 17, Paul views his imprisonment and possible death as a "drink offering." We need to look at the Old Testament offering which he refers to, so we can understand this picture. Read Numbers 15:8-10.

   (a) What was the main offering or sacrifice?

   (b) What was the "drink offering"?

3. (a) How had the Philippians' lives been ones of sacrifice and service?

   Philippians 1:29, 30

   Philippians 4:14-16

   (b) How had Paul's life been an offering? Acts 20:24

4. In light of what you've learned in questions 2 and 3, explain Paul's picture of his and the Philippians' lives in 2:17a.

5. (a) What was Paul's attitude and action in the giving of his life for Christ? (Verse 17b)

(b) What does he exhort the Philippians to
    do in the midst of theirs and his suffer-
    ings? (Verse 18)

(c) Why could Paul (and we) have this kind
    of attitude?
    Matthew 16:24-27

(d) Meditate on these things. Ask God to
    give you a heart like that and a mind set
    on the truth of Matthew 16:24-27.

(e) Is there any situation in your life in
    which you need to apply these truths?
    How?

(f) Praise and thank God for the privilege of
    losing your life for Him and the life in
    Him that you experience when you do.

19 But I hope in the Lord Jesus to send Timothy to you shortly, so that I also may be encouraged when I learn of your condition.

20 For I have no one else of kindred spirit who will genuinely be concerned for your welfare.

21 For they all seek after their own interests, not those of Christ Jesus.

22 But you know of his proven worth that he served with me in the furtherance of the gospel like a child serving his father.

23 Therefore I hope to send him immediately, as soon as I see how things go with me;

24 and I trust in the Lord that I myself also shall be coming shortly.

25 But I thought it necessary to send to you Epaphroditus, my brother and fellow-worker and fellow-soldier, who is also your messenger and minister to my need;

26 because he was longing for you all and was distressed because you had heard that he was sick.

27 For indeed he was sick to the point of death, but God had mercy on him, and not on him only but also on me, lest I should have sorrow upon sorrow.

28 Therefore I have sent him all the more eagerly in order that when you see him again you may rejoice and I may be less concerned about you.

29 Therefore receive him in the Lord with all joy, and hold men like him in high regard;

30 because he came close to death for the work of Christ, risking his life to complete what was deficient in your service to me.

1 2 3 4 5 6 7 8 9 10 11 12

TWO CHOICE MEN

Philippians 2:19-30

When circumstances begin to choke the life out of us, we're in need of spiritual and emotional CPR. We're in need of quality friends to breathe encouragement and stability back into our souls. At such times, the character of those we lean on becomes all important. Just as a drowning victim desperately needs a qualified rescuer to administer CPR, so we need friends filled with God's spirit and schooled in His ways to minister to us.

Paul was no exception. In his prison experience, he needed to be ministered to, and God didn't neglect him. Through two choice men, Timothy and Epaphroditus, God ministered deeply to his spirit. As Paul shares with the Philippians the details of his plans for these men, he gives us a glimpse into their characters. They were men who exemplified his exhortations in the first half of the chapter, who really lived out the life of Jesus Christ within them. They were men God could use on CPR assignments.

Study 1 – *Paul's Situation* (2:19-21)

1. Read the introduction and Philippians 2:19-30.

2. (a) What was Paul's desire? (Verse 19)

   (b) Why did he hope to do this (2a)? (Verse 19)

   (c) Why would Paul say this (2a) was a "hope in the Lord"?
   James 4:13-16 (especially verse 15)

   (d) Meditate on these things. What does this tell you about the desires of your heart and the plans you make?

3. (a) Why was the condition of these believers so important to Paul that he was willing to part with his dearest companion to hear how they were doing?
   1 Thessalonians 3:6-10

   (b) What further understanding of the oneness of believers that Paul mentions in Philippians 2:2 does this (3a) give you?

*4. (a) Why was Timothy the only one Paul could send to the Philippians? (Verses 20 and 21)

   (b) Compare the description of the Christians Paul knew in Philippians 2:20, 21

with Paul's exhortation to those in
Philippians 2:3 and 4.

5. (a) Prayerfully review your answers. Ask
    God to open your heart and life to His
    work.

   (b) How has your understanding/apprecia-
   tion of the Christian life and/or relation-
   ships of believers grown from your
   study?

   (c) Praise and thank God for the things you
   wrote down in 5b.

   (d) How do the truths you've learned need
   to affect your life as a member of the
   body of Christ? (Ask God for insight.)

Study 2 – *Timothy's Character and Mission (2:19-24)*

1. Read Philippians 2:19-30.

2. (a) What do you learn about Timothy from Philippians 2:19-23?

    (b) Meditate on these character qualities. Praise God for Timothy's life.

    (c) How is Timothy's life an illustration of Paul's exhortation in Philippians 2:3-8?

    (d) What character quality(ies) of Timothy do you need in your life? Why?

    (e) Ask God to work into your life what you write down in 2d. Praise and thank Him for what He's going to do.

3. (a) When was Paul going to send Timothy to Philippi? (Verse 23)

    (b) What did he hope for himself? (Verse 24)

*4. (a) Compare David and Jonathan's relationship in 1 Samuel 18:1-3; 19:1-7; 20:1-42; 2 Samuel 1:11, 12, 26 with that of Paul and Timothy in Acts 16:1-3; 1 Corinthians 4:17; 2 Timothy 1:3-6; 2:1-3; 4:9, 21; Philippians 2:19-23.

(b) What do you learn about close relation-
     ships from the examples of these men?

(c) How do the things you've learned about
     these relationships need to affect your
     closest relationships?

(d) If you don't have a close friend, ask God
     for one. Claim Ephesians 3:20.

Study 3 – *Epaphroditus' Character* (2:25)

1. Again read Philippians 2:19-30.

2. How does Paul describe Epaphroditus? (Verse 25)

3. (a) Why were Epaphroditus and Paul brothers?
Luke 8:19-21 (cf. Romans 8:29)

   (b) Meditate on this. Praise and thank God for the family you have as a new creature in Christ.

   (c) What does your family in Christ mean to you?

   (d) If you've never accepted Christ's gift of salvation, do so today.

4. (a) With whom were Paul and Epaphroditus working?
1 Corinthians 3:9

   (b) How is one a good worker or laborer with God?

   1 Timothy 4:7-10

   1 Thessalonians 1:3

   (c) Meditate on these truths. What stands out to you? Why?

(d) Asking God for insight, how do these
    truths need to affect your walk with
    God?

5. (a) How is one a good soldier of Jesus
       Christ?

   2 Timothy 2:3, 4

   Ephesians 6:10-18

   (b) Meditate on these things. What stands
       out to you? Why?

   (c) Asking God for insight, how do you
       need to be a better soldier?

6. Ask God to work in you what you wrote
   down in 4d and 5c. Praise and thank Him for
   what He's going to do (Ephesians 3:20).

Study 4 – *Epaphroditus' Service and Illness (2:25-28)*

1. Read Philippians 2:19-30.

2. How had Epaphroditus served Paul? Philippians 2:25; 4:18

3. (a) Why was Paul sending Epaphroditus back? (Verses 26 and 27a)

   (b) What had God done for Epaphroditus and Paul? (Verse 27)

   (c) What was Paul's desire in sending Epaphroditus home? (Verse 28)

   (d) Review your answers. What do these things tell you about the interrelationship between Christians?

   (e) Praise and thank God for the church, Christ's body on earth.

4. (a) What truth about God's mercy did Paul hang on to as his friend lay near death? Lamentations 3:21-25 (lovingkindness = mercy)

   (b) Meditate on these truths. Praise and thank God for them. What do these truths mean to you?

   (c) What situation do you have in which you need these truths to see you through?

   (d) Memorize Lamentations 3:21-25. Review it daily for six weeks. Meditate on it often.

Study 5 – *Epaphroditus' Honor* (2:29, 30)

1. Read Philippians 2:19-30.

2. (a) How were the Philippians to treat Epaphroditus when he returned? (Verse 29)

   (b) Why? (Verse 30)

   (c) How does Epaphroditus' life illustrate the truth found in John 12:25, 26 (cf. Matthew 16: 24, 25)?

   (d) Meditate on these things. How do these truths need to influence your thinking?

   (e) Praise and thank God for His faithfulness to His Word.

3. (a) How is Epaphroditus' life another illustration of Philippians 2:3-8?

   (b) Is your life an illustration of Philippians 2:3-8? How or how not?

   (c) Ask God to work in your life that you might ever be a deeper expression of Philippians 2:3-8. Thank Him for what He's going to do.
   Ephesians 3:20!

*4. (a) What is the basic theme of Chapter 2?

   (b) How does the whole chapter relate to that theme?

1 Finally, my brethren, rejoice in the Lord. To write the same things again is no trouble to me, and it is a safeguard for you.

2 Beware of the dogs, beware of the evil workers, beware of the false circumcision;

3 for we are the true circumcision, who worship in the Spirit of God and glory in Christ Jesus and put no confidence in the flesh,

4 although I myself might have confidence even in the flesh. If anyone else has a mind to put confidence in the flesh, I far more:

5 circumcised the eighth day, of the nation of Israel, of the tribe of Benjamin, a Hebrew of Hebrews; as to the Law, a Pharisee;

6 as to zeal, a persecutor of the church; as to the righteousness which is in the Law, found blameless.

7 But whatever things were gain to me, those things I have counted as loss for the sake of Christ.

8 More than that, I count all things to be loss in view of the surpassing value of knowing Christ Jesus my Lord, for whom I have suffered the loss of all things, and count them but rubbish in order that I may gain Christ,

9 and may be found in Him, not having a righteousness of my own derived from the Law, but that which is through faith in Christ, the righteousness which comes from God on the basis of faith,

10 that I may know Him, and the power of His resurrection and the fellowship of His sufferings, being conformed to His death;

11 in order that I may attain to the resurrection from the dead.

WARNINGS, EXAMPLES, AND EXHORTATIONS, Part 1

Philippians 3:1-11

An old man once said that it had taken him forty long years to learn three simple things. First, that he could do nothing to save himself. Second, that God didn't expect him to. And third, that Christ had done it all. This is also the testimony of Paul in Philippians 3:1-11. He exhorts the Philippians to rejoice in their God, for He alone had provided their salvation. He warns them of those who would pervert that truth. He then uses his own life as a living illustration of the truth he is emphasizing.

Paul had all the credentials a man needed in his day to "earn" right standing with God. But it wasn't enough. Paul knew that nothing was worth anything when it came to gaining a right relationship with God but the blood of Jesus Christ. When this truth sank into his heart, he found a new desire in life. His purpose was no longer to earn his way to Heaven, but to know and experience His Savior in every aspect of life.

Study 1 – *Rejoicing in the Lord* (3:1)

1. Read the introduction and Philippians 3:1-11.

2. Define rejoice.

3. (a) In whom are we to rejoice? (Verse 1)

    (b) Why?

    Psalm 27:1

    Psalm 32:8

    Psalm 33:11

    Psalm 68:5, 6

    Psalm 89:8-13

    Psalm 94:14

    Psalm 103:8-14

    Psalm 145:18, 19

4. Spend time rejoicing in your God.

5. Which truth in 3b particularly ministered to you? Why?

Study 2 – *True and False Believers* (3:2, 3)

1. Read Philippians 3:1-11.

2. (a) Who are the people described in verse 2?
        Acts 15:1; Galatians 6:12, 13

    (b) Why is Paul so hard on them?
        Galatians 6:14, 15; 2 Corinthians 11:13-15

3. In Romans 2:28, 29, we find that the "true circumcision" are true believers in Jesus Christ. Paul describes a true believer in verse 3.

4. (a) Define worship.

    (b) Why do we worship in the Spirit of God?
        John 4:23 and 24; Romans 8:9, 10

    (c) What do you discover about worshipping God from the psalmist's expression of worship in Psalm 63?

    (d) How do you need this (4c) in your life?

5. Why do Christians glory (boast) in Christ Jesus?

    Galatians 6:14

    1 Corinthians 1:30, 31

6. Why do Christians put no confidence in the
   flesh (human achievements) for salvation?
   John 6:63

7. Meditate on the truths you've learned today.
   Praise and thank Christ for who He is and
   what He's done.

8. What stood out to you in today's lesson?
   Why?

Study 3 – *Paul's Past* (3:4-8)

1. Again read Philippians 3:1-11.

2. The Jewish leaders boasted in their fleshly achievements under the law. In Philippians 3:4-6; Paul shares all the advantages of heredity and effort that he had under the law. If the Judaizers had something to boast about, they couldn't outdo him. But then in verses 7 and 8 Paul gives his conclusion to it all.

3. What is the significance of the things Paul boasted in?

    (a) "Circumcised the eighth day"
    Genesis 17:12 (cf. Genesis 21:4;
    Leviticus 12:3; Luke 2:21)

    (b) "Nation of Israel "
    Exodus 19:5, 6

    (c) "Tribe of Benjamin"
    Genesis 35:16-18; 1 Kings 12:21; Ezra 4:1

    (d) "Hebrew of Hebrews"
    Acts 6:1 (cf. 21:40—22:3)

    (e) "As to the Law, a Pharisee"
    Acts 26:5 (cf. Galatians 1:14)

    (f) "As to zeal, a persecutor of the church"
    Acts 26:9-11 (cf. Acts 8:1-3; 9:1, 2)

(g) "Righteousness which is in the Law,
found blameless"
Romans 10:2-5

(h) Review your answers. Ponder Paul's credentials. What stands out to you? Why?

4. (a) What did Paul conclude about these things (3a-g) when he met Christ (Acts 9)?
Philippians 3:7

(b) Why?
Galatians 2:15, 16; Matthew 5:20

(c) How did Paul view his life? (Verse 8)

(d) Meditate on these truths. What impressed you from these truths? Why?

(e) Is there anything apart from Christ that you're holding on to or trying to do to gain acceptance from God?

Study 4 – *Paul's Righteousness* (3:9)

1. Once more read Philippians 3:1-11.

2. What desire does Paul express in verse 9?

3. Righteousness is right standing with God. It is being in a right relationship to Him. It is being *all* that God requires a man to be.

4. (a) What is the righteousness that comes from the law (verse 9)?

    Romans 9:31, 32; 10:5

   (b) Why is this righteousness (4a) impossible to attain?

    Romans 3:19, 20
    Romans 4:14, 15
    Romans 10:3, 4

5. How does one become righteous?

    Romans 3:21-24 (cf. 2 Corinthians 5:21)
    Romans 10:6-11 (especially verses 9 and 10)

6. Are you righteous?

   (a) If not—accept Christ now.

   (b) If you are—praise and thank God for your righteousness. Ask God to deepen your appreciation of this *great gift* He's given you.

7. Meditate on these truths. What stands out to you? Why?

Study 5 – *Paul's Goal* (3:10, 11)

1. Read Philippians 3:1-11.

2. The righteousness Paul had in Christ put yearnings in his heart which he expresses in verses 10 and 11.

3. How does one come to know Christ deeper and deeper?

   John 14:21

   2 Corinthians 4:11

4. What is this resurrection power which Paul desires to experience in his life?

   Romans 6:4-11

   2 Corinthians 1:8-10 (cf. 4:7-10)

5. Why did Paul desire to fellowship in Christ's sufferings?

   2 Corinthians 1:3-5

   2 Corinthians 12:9, 10

   1 Peter 4:12-14

6. How does one live in conformity to Christ's death?

   Romans 6:12, 13

7. (a) These things (questions 3-6) Paul desires
in verse 10 have a goal which he states
in verse 11. Paul wanted to attain to the
resurrection from the dead. We know
from other Scripture that his bodily resurrection is assured (1 Corinthians 15).
The word Paul uses here for resurrection is not used anywhere else in the
New Testament. He is speaking of the
spiritual resurrection which he talks
about in Ephesians 2:4-7. Meditate on
its truths. Praise and thank God for
them. Ask God to work in you to live out
these truths.

*(b) How would experiencing the things Paul
desired in verse 10 achieve his desire in
verse 11?

8. (a) Meditate on the truths you've learned
today. Which one did God particularly
impress upon your heart? How?

(b) How does your life need to reflect these
desires?

12 Not that I have already obtained it, or have already become perfect, but I press on in order that I may lay hold of that for which also I was laid hold of by Christ Jesus.

13 Brethren, I do not regard myself as having laid hold of it yet; but one thing I do: forgetting what lies behind and reaching forward to what lies ahead,

14 I press on toward the goal for the prize of the upward call of God in Christ Jesus.

15 Let us therefore, as many as are perfect, have this attitude; and if in anything you have a different attitude, God will reveal that also to you;

16 however, let us keep living by that same standard to which we have attained.

17 Brethren, join in following my example, and observe those who walk according to the pattern you have in us.

18 For many walk, of whom I often told you, and now tell you even weeping, that they are enemies of the cross of Christ,

19 whose end is destruction, whose god is their appetite, and whose glory is in their shame, who set their minds on earthly things.

20 For our citizenship is in heaven, from which also we eagerly wait for a Savior, the Lord Jesus Christ;

21 who will transform the body of our humble state into conformity with the body of His glory, by the exertion of the power that He has even to subject all things to Himself.

WARNINGS, EXAMPLES, AND EXHORTATIONS, Part 2

Philippians 3:12-21

Every four years the world rivets its eyes on a special athletic contest. Countries around the globe send their best athletes to compete in the Olympic Games, and they watch expectantly as their countrymen strive to "bring home the gold." The dedication, perseverance, and single-mindedness of the contestants is obvious to even a casual observer. Wearing their national colors, the athletes compete as proud citizens of their homeland. Any rewards they receive bring glory not only to themselves, but also to the land they represent.

In Philippians 3:12-21, Paul likens the Christian life to the all-out effort of the Olympic Games. We are citizens of Heaven—the reputation of our homeland is on the line. The way we live needs to reflect our citizenship. Total Christlikeness is our goal. It will take determination and effort, but the "gold" we run for is well worth it—our Savior's presence, a "well done," and a new body.

May you be strengthened in your commitment to Christ as you study this week; may your heart be thrilled as you contemplate the "gold" awaiting you!

Study 1 – *Pressing On* (3:12-14)

1. Read the introduction and Philippians 3:12-21.

2. Last week you learned that the life Paul was desiring was experiencing fully the resurrected life he had in Christ. Today we'll discover how he went about accomplishing that desire.

3. (a) What does Paul say about his daily experience of the life he has in Christ? (Verse 12a)

    (b) What is he doing to achieve his goal? (Verse 12b)

    (c) Why? (Verse 12c)

4. (a) For what purpose did God lay hold on Paul's (your) life?

    Romans 8:29

    Ephesians 1:4

    Ephesians 2:10

    (b) What was Paul's evaluation of God's working out this purpose in his life? (Verse 13a)

(c) What was Paul's response to this evaluation? (Verses 13b and 14)

(d) How does one do this (4c)?
Hebrews 12:1, 2

5. (a) What is the prize Paul (we are) is waiting for?

Luke 19:17

1 Corinthians 2:9

1 Peter 1:4

Revelation 22:3, 4

6. (a) Spend time meditating on these truths. Ask God to renew your mind to think according to the true purpose and goal of your Christian life. Praise and thank Him for these truths.

(b) Which truth stood out to you today? Why?

*7. Summarize what Paul is saying in Philippians 3:12-14.

Study 2 – *Walking By the Pattern* (3:15-17)

1. Again read Philippians 3:12-21.

2. Yesterday you learned much about Paul's attitude in his Christian life. Review yesterday's lesson.

3. (a) What attitude does Paul command the Philippians (you) to have? (Verse 15)

   (b) If there is any area of their (your) life where they (you) aren't living by this attitude, what will God do? (Verse 15)

   (c) Prayerfully evaluate your life attitude in view of the truths you learned yesterday.

   (d) How has your life reflected these truths? (Praise and thank God for what He's done.)

   (e) Where do you need work? (Confess to God any disobedience, failure, as sin. Ask His forgiveness, and thank Him for it.)

   (f) Ask God to help you work what you wrote down in 3e deep into your life.

4. What are we to do with the light (understanding of ourselves and Scripture) we do have? (Verse 16)

5. (a) Who was to be the Philippians' model in
       the Christian life? (Verse 17)

   (b) Why could he say this?

       1 Corinthians 11:1

       Ephesians 2:19, 20

6. (a) Who has modeled the Christian life for
       you?

   (b) Praise and thank God for that person(s).
       How has their life helped you walk with
       God?

   (c) Send them a note of appreciation for
       their Christian example.

   (d) Who watches your life as a Christian
       (children, fellow workers, friends)?

   (e) Ask God to strengthen your walk in Him
       that others might see Christ in you.

Study 3 – *Enemies of the Cross* (3:18, 19)

1. Read Philippians 3:12-21.

2. (a) Who is Paul talking about in verses 18 and 19? (Verse 18b)

    (b) What is going to happen to them? (Verse 19a)

    (c) What are they like? (Verse 19)

3. What does it mean to say a person's god is their appetite?
    Luke 12:17-19; Romans 16:18 (cf. Isaiah 56:10-12)

4. What does it mean to say a person glories in their shame?
    2 Peter 2:18, 19 (cf. Revelation 18:7a)

5. What does it mean to say a person has their mind set on earthly things?

    Matthew 16:23 (cf. Romans 8:5-7)

6. (a) Review your answers. What stands out to you? Why?

    (b) What is Paul's attitude towards these people? (Verse 18a)

    (c) What is yours?

*7. (a) Compare Philippians 3:18, 19 with 2 Peter 2:1-3.

(b) Compare Philippians 3:18, 19 with Ephesians 2:1-3.

(c) What conclusions can you draw from your comparisons?

Study 4 – *Heavenly Citizenship* (3:20)

1. Read Philippians 3:12-21.

2. (a) Why were the Philippians to walk like Paul and not those described in verses 18 and 19? (Verse 20a)

   (b) What does this (2a) mean?

   Colossians 3:1-4 (cf. Ephesians 2:6)

   Hebrews 11:13, 16 (cf. 11:10; 13:14)

   *(c) What is our "homeland" like?
   Revelation 21:10-22:5

   (d) Meditate on these truths. Praise and thank God for them.

3. (a) What is our present attitude to be? (Verse 20b)

   (b) Why?

   Psalm 16:11

   Psalm 73:25, 26

   2 Peter 3:11-13

(c) Meditate on these things. Worship your Savior.

(d) Are these things true of your attitude? How or how not?

(e) Ask God to work in you to reflect these truths.

4. Which truth did you learn today that ministered to you most? How? Why?

Study 5 – *Divine Transformation* (3:21)

1. Read Philippians 3:12-21.

2. (a) What will Christ do when He comes for us? (Verse 21a)

    (b) How will He do it? (Verse 21b)

3. (a) What is Christ's heavenly body like?

    Luke 24:36-43 (cf. John 20:19-23)

    1 Corinthians 15:41-44

    (b) According to Philippians 3:21 and what you learned in 3a, what will your heavenly body be like?

    (c) Praise and thank God for these truths.

4. (a) Why does Christ have power to subject all things to himself?
    Ephesians 1:19-23

    (b) Meditate on these truths. Praise and thank God for them. Ask Him to make it a reality to you.

5. What stands out to you most from today's lesson? Why?

1 Therefore, my beloved brethren whom I long to see, my joy and crown, so stand firm in the Lord, my beloved.

2 I urge Euodia and I urge Syntyche to live in harmony in the Lord.

3 Indeed, true comrade, I ask you also to help these women who have shared my struggle in the cause of the gospel, together with Clement also, and the rest of my fellow-workers, whose names are in the book of life.

4 Rejoice in the Lord always; again I will say, rejoice!

5 Let your forbearing spirit be known to all men. The Lord is near.

6 Be anxious for nothing, but in everything by prayer and supplication with thanksgiving let your requests be made known to God.

7 And the peace of God, which surpasses all comprehension, shall guard your hearts and your minds in Christ Jesus.

8 Finally, brethren, whatever is true, whatever is honorable, whatever is right, whatever is pure, whatever is lovely, whatever is of good repute, if there is any excellence and if anything worthy of praise, let your mind dwell on these things.

9 The things you have learned and received and heard and seen in me, practice these things; and the God of peace shall be with you.

1 2 3 4 5 6 7 8 9 10 11 12

STANDING FIRM

Philippians 4:1-9

What we think on is the seed from which our life is reaped.

Most of us as children played "King of the Mountain." One child plants his feet firmly on the "mountain" and proclaims his sovereignty. All the rest of the children immediately attack trying to knock him off his "mountain." His feet must be firmly planted if he is to withstand their onslaughts.

As Christians we are given a heavenly kingdom with all the privileges of its citizenship. We are to proclaim to the world whose we are and His message of truth. All the forces of hell will try to batter us down, but in Philippians 4:1-9 Paul exhorts us to "stand firm in the Lord."

Our battle is not a physical one, but spiritual. To stand firm as royal children, we must continually rejoice in our King, live like Him, pray to Him, and think on Him. If we do, Paul promises that we'll experience deeply His presence and peace.

Your victory has already been won by your sovereign Lord. May you learn this week how to stand firm in it!

Study 1 – *In Unity* (4:1-3)

1. Read the introduction and Philippians 4:1-9.

2. (a) How does Paul feel about the Philippians? (Verse 1)

   (b) What does he desire for them? (Verse 1)

3. (a) What was the first step the Philippians (you) needed (need) to take to stand firm? (Verses 2 and 3)

   (b) Why would this (3a) be important? Matthew 12:25

   (c) Meditate on this truth. Pray for yourself and your church that you might stand strong together in unity. Pray for the church of Jesus Christ worldwide that it might stand strong in unity.

   (d) Ask God to convict you if there's any situation or any relationship in which you are not living in unity with your fellow Christians. Ask God for wisdom to know how to work out the situation or relationship harmoniously (James 1:5). Then obey what He shows you.

4. (a) What is the "book of life"? (Verse 3) Exodus 32:32; Revelation 20:12

(b) Whose names are in the "book of life"?
Luke 10:17-22 (especially verses 20 and
22); John 6:35-40 (cf. Hebrews 12:23)

(c) What will happen to those whose names
are not written in the "book of life"?
Revelation 20:15

(d) What will happen to those whose names
are written in the "book of life"?
Revelation 21 (note verse 27)

(e) Is your name written in the "book of
life"?

If not, accept Christ's salvation today.

If yes, rejoice (Luke 10:20).

(f) When was your name written in the
"book of life"?
Revelation 13:8 (cf. 17:8)

(g) Praise and thank God for your salvation.

5. What stood out to you most in today's lesson?

Study 2 – *In Rejoicing and Forbearing* (4:4, 5)

1. Read Philippians 4:1-9.

2. (a) What is the second thing Paul exhorts the Philippians and us to do in order that we might stand firm? (Verse 4)

   (b) When are we to do this? (Verse 4)

   (c) How can we do this?

      Psalm 34:1, 2 (cf. Psalm 145:1, 2)

      Romans 5:3-5 (cf. James 1:2-4)

      Hebrews 13:15 (cf. 1 Thessalonians 5:16-18)

   (d) Meditate on these truths. What stands out to you? Why?

   (e) Is there any situation in your life where you are not rejoicing in the Lord?

   (f) Confess as sin to God your disobedience in what you wrote down in 2e. Ask His forgiveness, and thank Him for it.

   (g) Spend time rejoicing in the Lord in what you wrote down in 2e.

(h) How have you been encouraged through
    obeying?

3. (a) What is the third thing we are to do to
       stand firm? (Verse 5)

   (b) How does one live like this?

       Luke 6:29-35

       Titus 3:1, 2

   (c) Why are we to live this way? (Verse 5b)

   (d) What does this (3c) mean?
       1 Thessalonians 4:16-5:2

  *(e) Compare Philippians 4:5 with James
       5:7-11.

  *(f) Compare Philippians 4:5 with 2 Peter
       3:8-14.

   (g) Meditate prayerfully on these truths.
       What stands out to you? Why?

   (h) Asking God for wisdom, how do these
       truths need to affect your life?

Study 3 – *In Prayer* (4:6)

1. Again read Philippians 4:1-9.

2. (a) As a Christian, what are you allowed to worry about? (Verse 6a)

   (b) What in your life are you to pray about? (Verse 6)

   (c) How can you live this (2ab) way? (Verse 6)

   (d) Meditate on these truths.

3. There are four aspects of prayer seen in this verse: (1) Prayer—a general speaking to God in worship and devotion, (2) Supplication—a humble entreaty for one's specific needs, (3) Thanksgiving—thanking God for who He is, for the present situation, and for what He's going to do, (4) Requests—emphasize the object or thing desired of God.

4. Why do we give thanks even for the things we worry about?
   Ephesians 5:20

5. What can you do when you don't know what requests to make of God in a difficult situation?
   Romans 8:26, 27

6. What do we know about God's answers to
   our prayers?
   Romans 8:28

7. Summarize from Philippians 4:6 what is the
   fourth way we are to stand firm in the Lord.

8. (a) What or who in your life are you worry-
       ing about?

   (b) Spend time with God praying, supplicat-
       ing, thanking, and requesting for what
       you wrote down in 8a. (You may want to
       review question 3.)

   (c) Take a 3 x 5 card. On one side write in
       big bold letters STOP. On the reverse side
       write out Philippians 4:6, 7. Carry it with
       you. Every time you start to worry take
       it out and read the STOP. Then turn it
       over and read Philippians 4:6, 7. Then
       once again practice Philippians 4:6.

9. What ministered to you most in today's lesson?

Study 4 – *In Peace* (4:7)

1. Read Philippians 4:1-9.

2. What is God's promise to those who obey the command of Philippians 4:6? (Verse 7)

3. (a) Define peace.

   (b) What is the "peace of God"?
        John 14:27 (cf. 16:33); Romans 15:13
        (cf. Galatians 5:22)

   (c) Why can we enjoy God's peace?
        Romans 5:1; 2 Corinthians 5:21

4. What does it mean when it says that God's peace "surpasses all comprehension"?
   1 Corinthians 2:14

5. Why can God's peace stand guard over our hearts and minds in Christ Jesus?
   Ephesians 1:19-22

6. (a) Meditate on these truths. Praise and thank God for His peace.

   (b) What does God's peace mean to you?

*7. Compare Philippians 4:6, 7 with Isaiah 26:3.

Study 5 – *In Mind and Action* (4:8, 9)

1. Read Philippians 4:1-9.

2. What is the fifth thing we must do if we are to stand firm in the Lord? (Verse 8)

3. The things listed in verse 8 are a test for every thought we entertain. The verse is written below as a test. Define the word that is underlined.

    (a) Is it *true?*

    (b) Is is *honorable?*

    (c) Is it *right?*

    (d) Is it *pure?*

    (e) Is it *lovely?*

    (f) Is it of *good repute?*

    (g) Is it *excellent?*

    (h) Is it *worthy of praise?*

4. What can you think on that will always pass this test? Psalm 19:7:11

5. (a) Ponder your answers. What stands out to you? why?

(b) Ask God to help you restructure your thinking patterns along these lines.

6. Write this test (3a-h) on a card. Place it on your refrigerator, mirror, or at work as a reminder to help you evaluate what you think on and restructure your thought patterns.

7. (a) How has studying verse 8 affected your thinking?

(b) It has been well said—
Sow a thought, reap an action
Sow an action, reap a habit.
Sow a habit, reap a character.
Sow a character, reap a destiny.

What we think on is the seed from which our life is reaped.

8. (a) What is the sixth thing we must do if we are to stand firm in the Lord? (Verse 8)

(b) What is the promise if we do? (Verse 9)

9. What impact has this lesson had on your life?

10. Memorize Philippians 4:4-9.

10 But I rejoiced in the Lord greatly, that now at last you have revived your concern for me; indeed, you were concerned before, but you lacked opportunity.

11 Not that I speak from want; for I have learned to be content in whatever circumstances I am.

12 I know how to get along with humble means, and I also know how to live in prosperity; in any and every circumstance I have learned the secret of being filled and going hungry, both of having abundance and suffering need.

13 I can do all things through Him who strengthens me.

14 Nevertheless, you have done well to share with me in my affliction.

15 And you yourselves also know, Philippians, that at the first preaching of the gospel, after I departed from Macedonia, no church shared with me in the matter of giving and receiving but you alone;

16 for even in Thessalonica you sent a gift more than once for my needs.

17 Not that I seek the gift itself, but I seek for the profit which increases to your account.

18 But I have received everything in full, and have an abundance; I am amply supplied, having received from Epaphroditus what you have sent, a fragrant aroma, an acceptable sacrifice, well-pleasing to God.

19 And my God shall supply all your needs according to His riches in glory in Christ Jesus.

20 Now to our God and Father be the glory forever and ever. Amen.

21 Greet every saint in Christ Jesus. The brethren who are with me greet you.

22 All the saints greet you, especially those of Caesar's household.

23 The grace of the Lord Jesus Christ be with your spirit.

1 2 3 4 5 6 7

8 9 10 11 12

FINAL THOUGHTS

Philippians 4:10-23

All of us have probably had someone challenge us with the penetrating question, "Why don't you practice what you preach?" Too often we talk a better line than we live. Paul closes his thank-you letter by practicing what he's been preaching. He's exhorted the Philippians several times to "rejoice in the Lord," and now he does just that. As he opens his heart in thanks for their generosity, he rejoices in God. He doesn't rejoice because he wasn't satisfied before, for he had learned the secret of contentment in any and every circumstance. No, his joy was in what God was doing in the Philippians' lives, and the delight of his heart was in their sacrificial giving. God had met Paul's need. He would meet every need of each one of His children. He could be counted on. All glory belonged to Him.

May God teach you of himself and the contentment to be had in Him.

Study 1 – *Learning Contentment* (4:10-12)

1. Read the introduction and Philippians 4:10-23.

2. (a) Who did Paul rejoice in because of the Philippians' gift to him? (Verse 10)

   (b) Why would he do this (2a)?
   James 1:17

   (c) Meditate on this truth.

   (d) What good gifts have you received?

   (e) Spend time rejoicing in the Lord because of His good gifts (2d) to you.

3. Why hadn't the Philippians been helping Paul? (Verse 10)

4. (a) What does Paul want the Philippians to be sure to understand about his joy in their gift to him? (Verse 11a)

   (b) Why could he say this (4a)? (Verse 11b)

   (c) Define learned.

   (d) Define content.

(e) Meditate on what you've learned.

(f) How content are you?

5. (a) What was the result in Paul's life because
of 4b? (Verse 12)

(b) What had been Paul's "school" for learning step by step the secret of contentment?

2 Corinthians 6:4, 5; (cf. 11:23-27)

Romans 16:1, 2 (cf. Acts 16:15;
1 Corinthians 16:18; Philemon 22)

(c) Meditate on the truths you've learned.

(d) What kind of "school" has God used to
teach you that you might learn contentment?

(e) Thank Him for what you wrote down in
5d. Praise Him for what He desires to do
and is doing in your life.

6. How has today's study affected your outlook
on your life?

*7. Compare Paul's experience as related in
Philippians 4:10-12 with Hebrews 12:7-11.

Study 2 – *The Secret of Contentment* (4:13)

1. Again read Philippians 4:10-23.
2. What was the secret of contentment which Paul had learned? (Verse 13)

3. Why is this possible?

   Isaiah 40:28-31 (cf. Isaiah 41:10)
   Luke 1:37
   Galatians 2:20
4. How is this possible?

   2 Corinthians 12:9, 10
   Ephesians 3:16

5. Meditate on these truths. Ask God to make them real to you. Praise and thank Him for them. What ministered to you most from these truths? Why?

6. (a) Review what you wrote down yesterday in 5d. Go over the truths you've learned today, thanking and praising God that they are a part of your school of learning contentment. Pray Ephesians 3:16 for yourself.

   (b) How has today's lesson helped you in learning to be content?

*7. From what you've learned the last two days, how could you help your children learn to be content in every circumstance?

Study 3 – *Generous Giving* (4:14-18)

1. Read Philippians 4:10-23.

2. (a) Though Paul had learned to be content in every circumstance because of Christ's strength within him, what did he want the Philippians to know about their giving to him? (Verse 14)

   (b) What was their past record of giving to him? (Verses 15 and 16)

3. Though he's been talking about their gifts to him, what does Paul assure them about his focus? (Verse 17)

4. (a) How does giving "profit" a person?

   Psalm 41:1

   Proverbs 19:17 (cf. Matthew 10:42; Hebrews 6:10)

   Matthew 25:34-40

   Luke 6:38

   2 Corinthians 9:6-8

   (b) Meditate on these truths. What stands out to you?

5. (a) What is Paul's condition because of the
       Philippians' gift? (Verse 18a)

   (b) How did God view their gift? (Verse 18b)

  *(c) From what you learned in question 4a,
       why could Paul say what he did in verse
       18b?

   (d) When you give according to the truths
       you learned in 4a, how does God feel
       about your giving?

   (e) Meditate on these truths.

6. How has your understanding and/or appreciation of God grown from today's study?

Study 4 – *Our Generous God* (4:19, 20)

1. Read Philippians 4:10-23.

2. (a) What promise of God does Paul give to you in verse 19?

    (b) What do you learn about God's supplying our needs from these Old Testament passages?

    Deuteronomy 2:1-7 (especially verse 7)

    1 Samuel 7:5-12 (cf. 2 Chronicles 20:1-30)

    1 Kings 17:1-16

    (c) Meditate on these truths. Praise and thank God for who He is. Which truth touched your heart? How?

    (d) How has what you've learned from these Scriptures encouraged you to trust God to supply all your needs?

3. (a) What was Paul's response as God met his needs? (Verse 20)

    (b) Spend time doing the same as Paul (3a). Ask God to make this the pattern of your life.

Study 5 – *Final Greetings* (4:21-23)

1. Once more read Philippians 4:10-23.
2. In verses 21 and 22, Paul sends greetings from himself and some of those with him.

   (a) Who are the "brethren" (verse 21) with Paul?
   Romans 9:3, 4

   (b) Who are the saints in "Caesar's household"? (Verse 22)
   Philippians 1:13, 14

   (c) How do Paul's "greetings" illustrate the truth he has been emphasizing about the unity of believers?

3. (a) What is Paul's benediction on the Philippians? (Verse 23)

   (b) What do you learn about this "grace" from the following Scriptures?

   1 Corinthians 15:10
   Ephesians 2:7
   Ephesians 2:8, 9
   1 Timothy 1:14
   1 Peter 5:5-7

   (c) Meditate on these truths. Praise and thank God for them.

   (d) How has your understanding and/or appreciation of God's grace grown from today's study?

A LOOK BACK

Review of Philippians

When we come to the close of a letter from a loved one, we enjoy going back and savoring the parts which meant most to us. As we come to the end of our study of Philippians, we want to do the same. This week we'll review and savor the book. We'll take a look at what God has taught us about joy in the Christian life, the unity we have as believers, the future that's awaiting us, and the Savior we treasure. Make it personal! What has God taught you? Which truths meant the most and why? You may want to reread the book daily and review your notes to help you.

May God open your heart in a special way this week to savor the things He's taught you.

Study 1 – *The Believer's Joy*

1. Read the introduction.

2. What truths about joy in the Christian life have been most significant to you in your study of Philippians? How? Why?

3. Praise and thank God for these truths.

Study 2 – *The Believers' Unity*

1. What truths in Philippians about the unity of believers has meant the most to you? How? Why?

2. Praise and thank God for His family, your family.

Study 3 – *The Believer's Future*

1. Share the significant truths from Philippians about your future as a Christian (on earth and/or in Heaven) which mean the most to you. Tell how and why they've affected your outlook.

2. Praise and thank God for these truths.

Study 4 – *The Believer's Savior*

1. Share the truths about Jesus Christ which stood out to you in your study of Philippians. Tell how they've affected your love and appreciation of Him.

2. Praise and thank the Father for your Savior. Praise Christ for who He is.

Study 5 – *Your Life*

1. What truth(s) has had the most significant impact on your life from your study of Philippians? How? Why?

2. Praise and thank God for all He's done in you.

GUIDELINES FOR LEADERS

You don't learn to be a discussion leader in a vacuum. The learning takes place in the doing—the trial and error, days of success and days that are not so successful. But God is faithful. He prods us to grow day by day, and I am thankful for that.

Let's take a look at some general principles of leading a discussion group and ways of organizing your women's Bible study. (I share these not as an "expert," but as one who is learning like you in the school of practical experience. I must also note that I am deeply indebted to Pat Smith, who has shared with me her years of experience in Bible Study Fellowship and as coordinator of the Women's Bible Study in my home church. I pray that you will find encouragement and assistance in the suggestions that follow.)

Ideas for Class Organization

1. Discussion Group/Lecture.

This works well in groups of twenty or more. The women can be divided into groups of eight to twelve. After the lesson is discussed in small groups, the ladies come together for a teaching time on the passage. Sample agenda:

    (a) Opening
        (announcements,
        singing, coffee time)   15 minutes
    (b) Discussion group time   1-1 hrs.
    (c) Lecture/teaching   30-40 minutes

You can vary the times to suit your needs. In this set-up, the teaching leader can meet with the discussion leaders beforehand to cover the lesson and pray together.

2. Discussion Group

This works best for small groups (8-15). The leader can give a small summary at the end of the discussion. The amount of time spent will depend on the needs and desires of your group. You will need at least an hour to cover the material.

Choosing Discussion Leaders

Here are some things to think about when choosing a leader: (1) A discussion leader must be committed to Christ and be willing to commit herself unconditionally to love the women in her group as unto the Lord. (2) Being a discussion leader costs in time and energy. (3) A discussion leader is *not* a teacher, but a *guide* of the discussion. Just because a woman is outgoing does not mean she will be a good discussion leader. A good discussion leader must be able to control her talking and focus on drawing out others. (4) A discussion leader does not need to be a Bible scholar, but evidence of maturity in Christ is very important.

Purpose of a Discussion Group

A discussion group has a threefold purpose. One is to strengthen it in Bible knowledge. The discussion helps to solidify what is learned in personal study. The discussion time also gives incentive to finish the lesson.

The second purpose is to build up the body of Christ. Strong bonds grow as we openly share our lives and pray for one another. When one shares how God is teaching her, it spurs the rest of the group on. As we share what God is doing in our lives, we stimulate one another to love and good deeds (Hebrews 10:24).

It is important in a discussion group to keep both of these purposes in focus and in balance. Each purpose must be equally important if there is to be success.

A third purpose is worship. We need to praise God together for what we've learned together of Him and His ways.

Practical Suggestions for Leaders

1. Personal Preparation

Our own personal time with God is the most important aspect of being a discussion leader. Leading a group is not so much "doing" the right thing as "being" the right person. The spirit we bring to the discussion time sets the tone. Our spirit is dependent on our times of quietness alone with God during the week.

As God works in our lives, and as we come to know Him, then we have something to share with the women. God is free to love and work through us. In no way do we have to be perfect or "have it all together." The women in the group need our honesty—our failures as well as our victories.

They need to sense the reality of our walk with God and His Spirit within us. We won't necessarily be conscious of this. Second Corinthians 3:18 says that as we look at Him He transforms us into His image by the work of His Spirit. Our responsibility is to spend time with Him in His Word. He'll be faithful to do His part and the women in the group will reap the benefit.

God's ministry is just that—His. He will be faithful in working through us as we are faithful in walking with Him—even if it seems like we're doing the five step, three steps forward and two steps back!

Prayer is a vital part of our preparation. As we pray specifically for the women and the discussion time, we have the joy of seeing God's power displayed in answered prayer. Prayer is also the key to unconditional love. We don't always feel loving. Loving takes time, energy, and self-sacrifice. Often there are women in the group who are difficult to love naturally. As we honestly pour out our souls to God in prayer (Psalm 62:8), we begin to experience God's transforming power in our love. It is important to remember that love is not just feelings. Often it is only as we take steps of obedience to God's Word to do the loving thing (reach out, spend time, forgive, listen, etc.) that our feelings are transformed. But it all begins with prayer.

Lesson preparation is another essential for the discussion leader. The better we know the lesson, the freer we are to guide the discussion and respond to the needs of the women.

Spend time daily in study. It helps tremendously. Then at the end of the week's review—a thorough review helps to solidify all we've learned.

2. Phone Calls

One way to be sensitive to the needs of the women is to call them periodically (every week or two). This takes a commitment of time, but is very rewarding. As we ask questions to get to know them, and share ourselves with them, a relationship grows. They have the opportunity to share their needs with us. If they're having difficulty with the lesson, we can give assistance. Everyone needs to be loved and cared for. Our phone calls are one way to show the women that we care.

3. Group Luncheons

A luncheon (maybe one every six weeks) gives the women in the group an opportunity to get to know each other better. They can be held in a home, at the church, or in a restaurant—variety is nice. Have some "get-to-know-you" questions to break the ice. "How did you meet your husband?" or "What do you look for in a friend?" A few questions are good to get the women to share their joys, hurts, and desires.

4. Opening

The impression a woman gets when she walks through the door to the study is crucial. A friendly smile and warm greeting are vital. She needs to know immediately that she is wanted. For many it is a very threatening experience. It is all important that each woman feels accepted and significant. This responsibility need not rest solely on the leader's shoulders. Recruit others to help.

(a) Name tags are a good tool to promote a warm atmosphere. Remembering a person's name is extremely important for their self-worth. But remembering a lot of names is difficult. Name tags will solve this problem and put everyone on a first name basis.

(b) One way to make a newcomer feel at home is to ask one of the regulars to see her through the day—sit with her, introduce her to others, be her friend.

(c) Coffee and goodies can help to create a warm atmosphere.

(d) Begin with a few worship choruses to help focus attention on the Lord. These should not be heavy hymns, but simple songs that turn our hearts to our Father and Savior.

5. Prayer Time

Spend the first fifteen minutes of the discussion time in sharing prayer requests and praying. Prayer helps to build strong cords of love among the women. As we pray for one another and see God's answers, our faith grows. Encourage the women to share not only physical needs but also spiritual and emotional ones. This is an important aspect in fulfilling the purpose of the discussion.

6. Guiding the Discussion

(a) As discussion leaders we must always remember that our purpose is to guide, not dominate. Our desire is to draw out what the women have learned in God's Word. The Bible is the authority; the Holy Spirit is the teacher. If we supply "the answers," it stops discussion. The women need to know that what they've learned is important to us. We all are in a sense teaching one another as we share what we've learned together.

(b) Allow the women to volunteer their answers. Don't be afraid to wait a few moments for them to respond. Asking someone for answers makes for dull discussion.

(c) We need to listen carefully to each woman. Eye contact is important to good listening. Our full attention needs to be focused on the one who is sharing. We must be careful not to interrupt her by words, mental wondering, or body movements.

(d) A warm and sincere response helps to assure a woman of her worth, and the worth of what she's shared. Here are some sample responses:

> "I appreciate that."
> "That's really encouraging."
> "I identify with that."
> "You really applied that truth."
> "That's great! I hadn't thought of that."
> "Thanks for sharing that."
> "You have a beautiful spirit."
> "Thanks!"
> "God really ministered that for you."

It is important to remember that the answers be *sincere.* Praise and appreciation are welcomed by all of us, but they must be sincere. We need to ask God to give us a genuine appreciation for the women and what they share.

(e) Sometimes to answer a question a woman will share a hurt or difficulty in her life. It's good at those times to stop and have someone pray for her specifically. Don't leave a hurt hanging—a short prayer helps lift the load. It also goes a long way towards building a loving, caring group.

140

(f) As discussion leaders it is best to let others answer first. The one exception is personal application questions. If the women seem hesitant to share openly, we may need to take the lead. Openness breeds openness. If we are willing to be honest and vulnerable, the women will be more apt to do the same.

(g) Open sharing does not mean gossip. To guard against this, do not share anything about another person that you wouldn't share if they were present. Open sharing is sharing our own personal joys or struggles—not someone else's.

(h) The discussion time should flow—neither rushing or dragging our heels. Dividing the lesson in half beforehand, and knowing what time we should arrive at the halfway point, can help in getting through the entire lesson in the time allotted. But we need to be sensitive to the Holy Spirit. There may be a question God has used deeply in a number of lives. Don't be afraid to spend the time needed. It is important to cover the entire lesson, but it is also important to allow the Spirit freedom to work. A real balance is needed here. We need to ask God for wisdom as we lead. If we see that there won't be enough time to finish all the questions, just cover the key questions. (Mark these out beforehand in your review.) Let the women know if they have questions on any that you've skipped, you'll be glad to cover them after the study is over.

(i) Keep a sense of humor. It is not a deadly serious task. We should enjoy our time together. As Proverbs 17:22 says, "A joyful heart is good medicine." Laughter is a wonderful part of our time together.

7. Possible Problems

You may be saying, "This all sounds nice, but what do I do if . . .?"

(a) What do I do with the extremely shy woman? Never force a shy woman to share. For some just sitting there takes all the courage they can muster. Putting pressure on them can scare them away. They need to be treated very gently. The phone calls can be great help. Ask them about the lesson and, if they share, let them know how much it meant. Then ask them if they'd be willing to share it with the group. Always remember to be sensitive to their fears and *gently* draw them out.

(b) What do I do with the woman who talks all the time? It is important to gently limit her contributions so all the women have a chance to share. One way to do this is to ask that someone who hasn't shared yet answer the question. It's important not to publicly reprimand an overly talkative member in the group. If it becomes a serious problem, talk with her outside of class. Maybe meet for lunch one day. Let her know how much you appreciate her input, and how valuable it is. Share with her that some of the women have a more difficult time opening up or have less knowledge. She could assist you by giving them a little more opportunity to participate. This is an area that needs to be bathed in our personal prayer time during the week.

(c) What if someone gives a "wrong" answer? Again, sensitivity is needed. Though we should never say "that's wrong," we shouldn't let a wrong answer pass without clarification. A couple of ways to handle this are: (1) solicit others to add their answers, then give a summary leaving out the incorrect answer; (2) go to God's Word. Open it up together and let it be the authority. Whether a woman's answer is correct or not, let her know she's appreciated.

(d) What if I'm asked a question I don't know? Don't panic. We don't have to "know it all." We can ask if anyone else in the group knows the answer. If not, we can let them know it's a good question, and we'll give more time and study to it during the coming week.

(e) What if someone asks a question or makes a statement that can lead to a tangent? Let them know, though it's an interesting topic, it will have to be pursued at another time—maybe at a luncheon if everyone seems interested.

(f) What if no one's done their lesson? Spend time doing some of it together.

8. Evaluating Your Time

The best time to evaluate how your discussion group is doing is *NOT* right afterwards. Usually we're tired then, and that always colors the thinking. Sometime during the week check up on yourself:

> Is there a warm atmosphere?
> How's the timing coming?
> Am I being open? Are the women?
> Was I prepared?
> How are my listening skills?
> Are my shy gals sharing more?
> Are the talkers under control?

Don't just zero in on the negatives. Praise and thank God for the positives and progress. Ask

Him for wisdom in the areas that need work. Remember, He is growing us in this area of ministry. Thank Him for the privilege; thank Him for using you.

The Lesson

In discussing the lesson, it is not necessary to discuss every question. In the preface to the study the types of questions are listed. Most of the #1 questions and some of the #2 questions can be summarized by you, or can be covered by going quickly around the circle. The #3 and #4 questions make for the best discussion.

At the end of some sections, there is a question like, "What stood out to you most in this section." Instead of going through all the questions and then going back over them again in personal sharing, cover the section with that one question. But in doing this, it is important that the women tie their personal sharing in with the specific question, verse, and answer that stood out to them.

To begin the discussion time, you may want to use the introduction of the lesson as your springboard. You can pull out a point, summarize it, share something that stood out to you, or ask the women what stood out to them. The introduction can help bring into focus where you're going as you start the discussion time.

Remember to write any notes you need in your book so you can easily guide the discussion. Mark the key questions for discussion with a see-through marking pen. Some of the questions for discussion follow "Meditate . . ." or "Pray. . . ." Just cover the question part in discussion.